# TRIAL
## of a CITY
*and Other Verse*

# TRIAL
# of a CITY
## and Other Verse

## EARLE BIRNEY

THE RYERSON PRESS · TORONTO

*Published, September, 1952*

## PUBLISHER'S NOTE

The Indian Headman and his relatives in *Trial of a City* are characters of fiction, based upon a general study of the West Coast Salish in early days, and no reference is intended to any actual persons, living or dead.

## ACKNOWLEDGMENTS

Grateful acknowledgment to reprint some of the following poems is made to: *Arena* (N. Z.); *Canadian Forum; Canadian Home Journal; Contemporary Verse; Dalhousie Review; Here & Now; Mayfair; Northern Review; Outposts* (England); *Poetry Commonwealth* (England); *Saturday Night.*

FOR BOB AND RITA

# Contents

# Contents

# TRIAL of a CITY

*and Other Verse*

## I. TRIAL OF A CITY

A Public Hearing into the Proposed
Damnation
OF
Vancouver

*Place:* a small hall in the basement of the Vancouver Court-House

*Time:* five years later

*Characters and Ghosts:*

T. V. Announcer
Minister of History, Freed State of Columbia
Clerk of the Hearing
P. S. Legion—counsel for the Metropolis of Vancouver
Gabriel Powers, Q.C.—counsel for the office of the Future
Miss Take—stenographer
Captain George Vancouver—discoverer of Burrard Inlet
Sk'-wath-kw'-tlath-kyootl—Headman of the Snow-kwee Salish
Dr. E. O. Seen—professor of geology, U.B.C.
J. C. Deighton—Gassy Jack of Gastown
Long Will of Langland—author of *Piers Plowman*
Mrs. Anyone—housewife

ANNOUNCER—Ready, Mr. Minister?

MINISTER—Right.

ANN—We will begin televising in ten seconds from—now.

MIN—Drat, where's my gavel?

1

CLERK—O dear—O, there it is, sir, under that file.

MIN—Ah. Thanks. Ready.

ANN—We're . . . on . . . the . . . *air*.

MIN—By the powers conferred on me as Minister of History, I hereby convoke, on this seventh day of May, Nineteen Whatever-it-is, in the Metropolis of Vancouver, Freed State of Columbia, a Public Hearing to consider objections to the proposal to—eliminate the said Metropolis. Notice of objection has been filed with my Ministry, perhaps understandably, by the Metropolis itself, which is represented here today by its Counsel, Mr. P. S. Legion. The proceedings are being broadcast, televised, taped, taken down and otherwise recorded. And now let's get on with it. Mr. Legion, if you've anything to say on behalf of Vancouver, this is the time.

LEGION—Really, Mr. Minister, this seems to me irregular.
> I dont know what you're pulling, but I hope it's not our leg
> you are.

MIN—Come now, Mr. Legion, I know this isnt a Court of Law, but even in a Public Hearing you might preserve a little private dignity.

LEG—What's the use of dignity? And how can we discuss?
> Why there isnt any public here but us!

MIN—No confidence in your clients, Mr. Legion? Some of them, surely, are viewing us at this moment. You wouldnt expect any of them to come down to this Court House cellar when any chair at home would be softer. At any rate I'm here, and you're here, and opposing counsel, and the clerk and the stenographer. Everything's beautifully regular.

LEG—Regular? ! When someone is proposing, sir,
> (And no one *has* said who)
>> To eliminate my clients?
>> Who wants to—is it you?

MIN—I? Of course not, I'm neutral. The proposal comes from—a certain department.

LEG—Certain! *Un*certain! Department of what?
　　Department of Clambakes? Department of Thought?

MIN—Neither. A—an office in our ministry.

LEG—Of *course*—yours is the only one,
　　　You've swallowed all the others!
　　But—the Offices for Rockets, sir,
　　　For Rain, or Childless Mothers?

MIN—No, you wouldnt guess; it's a brand-new one—the Office of the Future.

LEG—What's this, sir? Who runs it? And why arent they here?
　　I protest for my clients. This is all very queer.

MIN—Naturally there's no one present from the Future. But our learned Queen's Counsel, Mr. Gabriel Powers, is here, of Queendom, Powers, Prince and Policy. You hold a brief for the Office of the Future, I believe, Mr. Powers?

POWERS—Yes, sir, a watching waiting all-too-brief.

LEG—What's this? . . . You're waiting, Mr. Powers? It's we who wait
　　To learn what grisly unnatural fate
　　You plan for our city, and when, sir, and why?

POW—Somewhen the Future will, and no why sooner,
　　　damn most god-naturely Vancouver.

LEG—What's that? I didnt catch—'damn,' did you say? Dam?
　　God-naturely? !

STENOGRAPHER—Please, Mr. Minister—

MIN—Language, Mr. Legion—ladies present!

LEG—*I* didnt say it first; I just wanted to know which—

STEN—Please, sir—

MIN—Yes, Miss Take, what is it?

STEN—How am I to spell—that word?

LEG—That's all *I* wanted to know.

MIN—A fair question. Mr. Powers?

3

Pow—With a d - a - m and an -n, or spell it dim, or doom, it is damnation we purpoise.

Leg—Pur—purpoise? !  You said—

Pow—Purpoise.

Sten—How do I spell—?

Min—Dont bother, Miss Take.   Leave Mr. Powers to the TV and the tape.

Leg—Look—what's all this doubletalk?

Pow—We poise our purpose, since our Judgment Deed's as yet undated.

Leg—Let's talk plain English.   I want a straight answer to—

Min—I'm afraid, Mr. Legion, you'll have to cash Mr. Powers' words at par.   Mr. Powers has been briefed by the Office of the Future and must use its language.   It's not his fault if English changed again.

Leg—I dont care what he talks, he must give us a reason!
    Our country's largest city—destroy it?   Why that's—*treason ! !*

Pow—Treason or true, the Office of the Future
    finds this city-pretty now a misfate
    in its planes.   Like every think of booty,
    sir, it's copulated to destriction;
    its lifeliness decreases and must ever
    pass into nothingmist.   Your town's dimnition
    is, I fear, both inevoidable and everdue.

Leg—My learned friend speaks gibberish
      To hide a government plot.
    But my two million clients will insist
      He tell us all what's what.
    It's rumoured an Order-in-Council was passed
    To experiment here with a z-bomb blast.
    The Premier's in hiding, the Legislature too.
    And now you talk of dims and dams—what *are* you going to do?

4

Pow—The V-Dayls of the doomning, Mr. Legion,
    are not yet warred out foully.
    Nor would it be within the public inrest
    to diverge them now.

Leg—This Hearing's all a farce.
    If you cant tell us clearly why
    Or how or when you plan to damn
    You've got no right to try.

Min—O, now, Mr. Legion, let's get on with it. This Hearing is to consider objections to the plan, not to the planners. The Future has the right, you know, to damn.

Leg—Right? Who gave it to them?

Min—The Ministry of History.

Leg—But, sir, that's you! *You're* biassed too. I demand another venue.

Min—There is no other. This must do. Please order from the menu.

Leg—My clients do not think, sir, this is a laughing matter.

Min—No more it is—for them—so let's cut out the chatter.

Leg—Now who's undignified? My clients, sir, object—

Min—My dear Mr. Legion, we know they object. But is any unbiassed person ready to support their objections?

Leg—I've thirty waiting in the ante-room
    Of every one of whom Vancouver's proud:
    The Mayor, ten bankers and five lumbermen,
    A champion lightheavyweight and—

Min—Sorry, not allowed.

Leg—What?

Min—Obviously biassed persons. They're all, technically at least, alive.

Leg—A—alive? Well, of course—what ! ?

5

MIN—My Ministry has ruled that only the dead are neutral. Or the newly born. Anyone not counted in last year's census. Have you none such to testify on behalf of your clients? No dead?

LEG—Of course I havent any dead! O this is ridiculous—insane! Illegal! I—I wont go on! You—

MIN—Temper, temper, Mr. Legion. Everything will be all right. As Minister of History I'm empowered to revive the dead for purposes of giving testimony. They'll have to fade away as soon as they've finished, of course, and I'd prefer not to have more than one of them standing around at a time. Now, who would you like to start with?

LEG—Who? How can I—

MIN—You'll find they've all been following the case. The dead havent anything else to do but look on. And they'll be glad to have a chance to talk again.

LEG—But—but—I dont know any dead!

MIN—What, none?

LEG—Well, none I'm sure would—that is—er—would—

MIN—Be on your side? I begin to think you lack faith in your case as well as in your clients, Mr. Legion.

LEG—It's not that at all, sir. It's just—I'm not prepared. I'll need a recess to—

MIN—Recesses not allowed. Besides, your chances are as good as Mr. Powers'. Even the Future's lawyer cant be certain what the Past thinks.

POW—Nor what the Present thinks is certain to be Future.

MIN—If you'd like a suggestion, Mr. Legion—why not start with your clients' namesake?

LEG—Who, sir?

MIN—Captain George Vancouver. I'm sure we'd all be interested in his comments.

6

LEG—Hmm, well—(*Suspicious*) you've already been talking to him?

MIN—I assure you, no. He's a virgin witness.

LEG—O all right—but I reserve notice of appeal.

MIN—Will the Clerk of the Court please ask Captain Vancouver to materialize?

CLERK—(*Calling*) Captain Vancouver! Captain Vancouver! Please materialize this way.

CAP V.—Aye, aye sir. Coming.

MIN—Welcome back, Captain. Mr. Legion here would like to ask you some questions.

CAP V.—Your sarvant, sir. Fire away.

LEG—You—you really are Captain George Vancouver?

CAP V.—That I am.

LEG—I'm honoured to meet you, Captain. And my congratulations.

CAP V.—Congratulations?

LEG—You sir, discovered Burrard Inlet around which the mighty city towers which bears your name. You may proudly boast you were our first white citizen, I think?

CAP V.—I happened to explore the inlet, true,
  (I think that was in seventeen ninety-two)
  Met savages, and from their eyes assumed
  We were the earliest who had presumed.

LEG—You were indeed. And now, Captain, tell us—

MIN—Excuse me, Mr. Legion, I dont quite follow your witness. Did you say Captain, you knew you were the first whites from the Indians' *eyes?*

CAP V.—I saw no glint of terror in their glance.

MIN—Ah, of course. Sorry, Mr. Legion. Carry on.

LEG—Well now, Captain. Arent you horror-struck to learn of these threats to end the beautiful city you began?

POW—A loaded question, Mr. Leading, but no matter.

CAP V.—Did I begin it?  Faith, it was by chance.
   My orders were to chart the northwest main
   And find if any strait led home again.
   I had to navigate the lot to say
   If none reached somehow back to Hudson's Bay.
   Bemused with this I never, more's the pity,
   Discerned along those shaggy cliffs a city.

LEG—I see you're modest, captain, but I'm sure
   You're glad to see the names of all your friends
   Living forever round your city's shores—
   (Unless this government contrives their ends).

CAP V.—Egad, old Atkinson would love the light
   You throw to sailors from his Point at night,
   And Grey would be dumfounder'd at those rows
   Along *his* Point of glass palazzios
   Your nabobs built; they have an outré charm.

LEG—I hope you've looked around our U.B.C.,
   Canada's fastest growing university,
   Complete—from atom-smashers to a farm—
   Bigger than Oxford; and the co-eds—say!

CAP V.—Almost as fetching as the girls in my day.

LEG—Ten thousand science grads a year!

CAP V.—But only twenty humanists, I fear.

LEG—Well—what about our port, that every captain praises;
   You wouldn't like to see *it* blown to blazes?

CAP V.—Old Burrard doubtless swells to know his harbour
   Is toothed with spars and docks from lar- to star-board.
   But all the town, those gross mechanic jaws
   That clamp and champ around your port—what was
   Your question, sir, again?

POW—You can load a captain to the water but you cant make him sink.

MIN—Mr. Legion wants to know, captain, if you object to the city's
face being, er, lifted.

LEG—Really, Mr. Minister, I must protest this levity.

MIN—Do please go on; my aim was only brevity.

LEG—My question, captain, was
    If you would wish to see
    This great metropolis,
    The west's unique Acropolis,
    Blown up, blown down, H-bombed, Z-bopped,
    Or otherwise wrecked utterly?

POW—Your question's once again misleading-loaded, Mr. Logion. Our method of bombnation's not yet settled. However, let the captain pray praycede.

CAP V.—Hmmm. I'm not the sort who likes to see things go—
    But what I saw, sir, went some time ago . . .
    Those paddling Indians who held a forum
    Around our boats—with what a proud decorum
    They shared their feast with us (some smelts they'd cooked).
    Their chief sat like Apollo bronzed, yet looked,
    Poor soul, on me as if I were the god.
    It seems his race are mostly under sod.

LEG—O no, we've hundreds yet, and some
    Gut fish for our great canning trade;
    Some wards of the state, but Christians all
    And voters—sure, they've made the grade.

POW—Objaculation, Mr. Minister! My wordy friend
    sleeks to mislead the captain into thinking-thanking
    bleak is white or grade disgrade, and every needive snug
    in his Prochristean bed.

MIN—Captain Vancouver seems able to form his own judgments, Mr. Powers. However, we might, later on, call up that decorous Apollo himself and get the Indian's story.

LEG—I object, sir. The Siwashes are a side issue.

MIN—Mr. Powers?

Pow—An excellent propuzzle, sir, most aboriginal. Let's have him
    soon.

Min—Right. Meantime, please continue Mr. Legion.

Leg—Look Captain, it's us whites that really matter;
    We built this mighty city in your name:
    Three generations hacked it from the timber—
    You wouldnt want to see it end in flame?

Cap V.—A feat indeed in such a trifling time
    To piece together so much wood (and grime);
    Tis big as my old London, and as dun,
    As planless, not so plaguey, but less fun.
    I rather liked the sweep of fir and cedar.
    Your city, sir—I cant think why I'd need her.

Leg— . . . Very well, Captain. Your witness, Mr. Powers.

Pow—Thank you, Mr. Legion,
    but you've performed all cross-examinations necessary
    and the Captain's made his story history.
    The Moby jaws, straining the plankton of our world,
    felt barb—O whale-a-way—
    rash-rushed upon this coast-not-understood.
    Caught in his tow came Captive Ahab here
    and gained a name; but for a habitation
    sliced fast the rope and left his great Albino
    beached forever, prime *immobile*.
    Then quickly White Dick swelled, with death-in-life
    grew flabby-puffed, delaquiescent,
    over the murmuring pains and the homelocks wept
    his sides, and dried to this framed abstract of a self,
    a prone bone lattice and a phosphoring city.
    The Future then need ask the nimble Captaive nowhat;
    he cut and ran long since, and never planned nor recks
    this beaching, never cares that we have come to
    bury Moby not appraise him.

MIN— . . . Well then, the Clerk will please de-materialize Captain Vancouver. Thank you, Captain.

CLERK—(*Sing-Song*) Captain Vancouver, please de-materialize this way.

CAP V.—(*Fading*) Your sarvent, gentlemen, and safe harbourage.

———  ———  ———

MIN—We'll proceed to your next witness, Mr. Legion. Who shall we pick this time from history's pocket? Simon Fraser? A missionary? Miner? An early Mayor, perhaps?

LEG—Mr. Minister, I must protest procedure so unfair.
I've got no time to quizz these ghosts in private, and prepare.

MIN—O now you want to make everything dull and logical. Always remember that Mr. Powers is under the same disadvantage.

LEG—Well let him call a witness, while I think.

POW—Agreed. But if it's seemly-same to you, sir, as Crown Sill
for the Future I prepare to hear and hire the Past not question
it. I'll leave the intercorruptions to opprosing Counsel.

MIN—Very well. That gives you leave to cross-question whenever you like, Mr. Legion.

LEG—Humph.

MIN—Call the Headman of the Snow-kwee Salish, 1792.

CLERK—Headman, Snow-kwee Salish, 1792, please materialize this way.

CHIEF— . . . Peace to my cousins.

CLERK—Name please.

CHIEF—Sk'-wath-kw'-tlath-kyootl.

CLERK—Sk'—who?

STEN—Please, sir, how am I to spell that?

CHIEF—Call me chief.

CLERK—(*To Steno*) Chief. C-H-E-I-F.

STEN—Thanks.

MIN—Welcome, Chief.   You met Captain Vancouver and were headman
when he sailed into Burrard Inlet?

CHIEF—And fifty summers more, after he sailed away.
    In the green shooting of my chieftainship the Captain's cloud-
        boat came,
    after the Rain Moon when we set the Chief my father
    high on a hemlock crotch in his canoe, within our burial wood.

MIN—We're presuming, Chief, you've kept abreast of happenings around
the Inlet since your own death.

CHIEF—I have watched, sir, the snow of my people melt
    under the white man's summer.

MIN—And you understand the issues being debated at this Hearing?

CHIEF—Where once we hunted, white men have built many longhouses,
    but they are uneasy as mice within them.
    They have made slaves of waterfalls
    and magic from the invisible dust of rocks
    and are stronger than grizzlies—
    but their slaves bully them,
    and they are chickadees in council.
    Some of you say: give them time, they will grow wise and find
        peace.
    Others say: the sun slides into the saltwater;
    they must follow the Indian into the trail of darkness.

MIN—Any objections to this summation, gentlemen?

POW—Object to such objectiveness?   Hidman, toll your story.

LEG—Well *I* object!   How could he understand?
    A primitive, a redskin, a pagan stone-age man!

MIN—Chief, do you feel capable of advising us?

CHIEF—We are all sons of the same brown Asia men.
    My fathers, roaming ever eastward,
    crossed over and made human half the world.

Your fathers, whitening over Europe,
and ever westering, circled back to us.
They walked with Powers of lead and steel
we had not known, unknowing had not lacked.
But bringing brought us need.

LEG—O come you always needed us; we had the know-how.
Without the white, the Indian was a lowbrow.

CHIEF—Before the tall ships tossed their shining tools
to us, my uncle was our carpenter.
With saw of flame he laid the great cedars low,
split the sweet-smelling planks with axe of slate,
bowed them his way with steam and thong,
shaped the long wind-silvered house
where thirty of my kin and I lived warm as bear and lusty.
He made it tight against the rain's long fingers,
yet panelled to let in the red-faced sun.
He hollowed the great canoes we rode the gulf in safe as gulls.
My uncle knew the high song of the cedar tree;
he had a Guarding Power with Brother Wood.

LEG—You got along somehow—that's all you really mean.
But honest now, you had it tough until we hit the scene.
For instance, is it true or not
You fellows couldnt even make a pot?

CHIEF—The tides bore in unasked our kelp-float flagons;
flint gave us fire, and earth and stones our ovens.
Red roots and yellow reeds entwined themselves within
our women's hands, coiled to those baskets dancing
with the grey wave's pattern or the wings
of dragonflies you keep in the great cities now
within glass boxes.   Now they are art, white man's tabu,
but once they held sweet water.

LEG—Give me an aluminum pressure-cooker any time.

13

CHIEF—It is swift indeed, as lava-springs,
    but it does not have our wave-pattern.

LEG—That's all very well, the things you'd eat.
    You never learned to farm; just wolfed raw fish and meat.

CHIEF—The wild lilies grew their pungent bulbs unprompted,
    the vines unfurled their green shoots for the plucking.
    The children dried our currants from the saskatoon,
    made cakes of strawberry, jam from the lush salal.
    My father and I were hunters for the longhouse.
    He taught me to bend a yew-bow, with snakeskin tape it taut,
    whittle arrows wind-light from the cedar,
    feathered, and agate-tipped.
    At night we would return with deer from the mountains
    or ducks glistening from the still shore-coves.
    Sometimes, gliding hushed on the sea,
    I would raise my lance, my quartz blade shining,
    hurl it home into a fat black porpoise;
    or with my horned harpoon snare Brother Seal.
    Then all the longhouse would make music,
    there would be roasting of the spiced roots,
    there would be sweet small plums,
    the shell-spoons would dip and glitter from the carved feasting
      bowls.

LEG—You're just remembering each trickier dish.
    Most of the time I'll bet it was fish.

CHIEF—There were bright days when all my village paddled,
    racing the wolfhead canoes to a rippled beach.
    The heady seasmell rose from glowing stone-pits;
    Then we held crab- and clam-feast,
    lay in talk till the beachfires came alight
    in the seas of the sky.

LEG—Sure, one day a feast and the next day a famine.
    I'm told you'd have starved if there hadnt been salmon.

CHIEF—Salmon was bread.
> When in the Moon of Blossoms the first silverback
> threshed in our basket-traps, my father's drum
> called all the village.
> The red flesh flaked steaming from the ceremonial spit.
> My father gave thanks to the Salmon Power,
> and everyone tasted bird-like.   Then we young men
> ran to the water with trolls and seine-nets.
> The bows of our canoes returning were flecked like mica.
> With flying fingers the women split the shiny ones,
> hung them on cunning cedar racks;
> our friends, the air and the sun,
> sealed the good oils for the winter storing.
> Salmon was bread.
> But my brothers could fashion bone-hooks
> strong as the wolf's jaw to grip the great river-sturgeon.
> Every year came the cod and the sea-trout to their hands,
> their nets boiled with shoals of the candlefish.
> It was not till your time, sir,
> I saw a Salish go hungry.

LEG—Humph.

POW—You have been faithfully unsirred, my leer-ed friend.

LEG—You're falling for a corny Hiawatha line.
> I'm through with this witness; he's wasting our time.

POW—All time's a waste of Hiawathas.
> Let this brown whiteness, Mr. Minister, tell on *his* time and waste.

MIN—Very well, but he might perhaps keep closer to the point.

POW—Our wheatman's present is impaled upon his village point.   He
lived as long, ate better.

LEG—My learned friend sets highest store
> By what goes down our throats.
> I'm defending civilization
> Not a camp of fishing boats.

15

CHIEF—There was something, I do not know,
  a way of life that died for yours to live.
  We gambled like fool-hens but we did not steal.
  My father spoke to the people always what was true.
  When there was quarrel, he made us speak it out in reason,
  or wrestle weaponless on the clean sand.
  We kept no men as warriors, we held no state on others.
  Each in his village had his work, and all made certain all
  were fed.

LEG—A village fit only for stone axes—
  No state, no money, and—

POW—No taxes?   An able Eden, Mr. Legion, without Cain.

LEG—It's taxes build a city, make a nation in the end.
  These fellows never learned defence because they'd nothing to
  defend.

MIN—Isnt your memory being a little kind, Chief?   Surely there were
  wars.

CHIEF—It is true the Kwakiutls would come like sea-wolves
  riding their war-canoes, raiding for slaves,
  and we could resist only as wrens flying.
  My grandmother fell by the woods' edge
  as she ran from their arrows.

LEG—You see!   The noble Siwash habits—
  When the enemy showed, you ran like rabbits.
  If the whites hadnt come there isnt a doubt
  The Kwaks would have cleaned the lot of you out.

CHIEF—The Kwakiutls were warriors and were quickly gone;
  they went looking for braves more worthy to conquer.
  With the long years they dwindled.
  It was our people who grew like the grey geese.
  When we paddled to others it was only to visit;
  our young men lived to be old.

16

LEG—But that wasnt any way to build security.
      You people never got things straight.
      You never thought in terms of *government.*
      You should have tried a tribal super-state.

CHIEF—Each summer the salmon came, the deer were plump in the
      river groves.

LEG—Sure, all you wanted was to hunt and eat.
      You never got much farther than the cave.
      But we've a culture built on art and—and thinking,
      A city worth our while to save.

CHIEF—Sometimes a young man would be many months in the woods
          thinking, alone as a heron,
      and learning the powers of the creatures.
      I lay and watched the little grey doctor, the lizard;
      I studied the spirit of bear; I came by their songs.
      When I was chief I carved Brother Bear on my houseposts,
      took the red earths and the white and painted his strength.

LEG—Gentlemen, you see—superstition, totem, tabu!
      This testimony's worthless, it's all a lot of voodoo.

CHIEF—It is true we saw marvels in each life,
      and wished to learn the eagle's dignity, the beaver's wisdom.
      It is true we had no ceremonies of blood-drinking,
      and we did not think of Jehovah.
      These, and Hell, the white man brought us.

LEG—Objection Mr. Minister.   This is a Christian Court.
      He's got no right to make such cracks.   It's time we cut him short.

MIN—Umm, well, this is a Hearing not a Court, Mr. Legion—the
      witnesses are not sworn.   However, if you've no more questions—

LEG—Wait—yes, I have.   Chief, will you tell us, pray,
      If all you Siwash—

CHIEF—Salish, please.

17

LEG—Well, if all you Salish were so smart
  How come you threw your goods away?
  Potlatches! Remember? Give your shirt off your back
  And beg for another the very next day?

CHIEF—Once our kindred gathered from many villages.
  Like dolphin they came arching over the waves.
  My father stood tall on the house-roof, called each by name,
  threw down a soft cloak of marten and mink,
  white rug of the wild goat's wool,
  or shaggy leggings of bearskin,
  tossed down for the catching red capes of the cedar bark,
  blankets woven with the woodpecker's colours,
  tanned shoes of deerhide, and root-mats
  brown as the last cloud in the sun's downgoing.
  The men made jokes, there was loon-laughter of women,
  we boys ran races over the hot sea-sand.
  After, by the full tide's brim,
  the Dance.
  My father put on the great-eyed mask of his Owl Power;
  with his secret kelp-whistle he talked owl-talk as he swayed.
  My uncle held his drum close to a tidepool,
  rubbed the skin cunningly with his hands,
  made the downy whoosh of the owl's wings in the night air.
  There was one who drew frog-talk from cockle-shells
  hidden in the pool of his fingers.
  The old men sang of wise chiefs that had been, and their spirits,
  the songs dying slowly as wind, then swelling
  as the board-drums beat tremolos, as the carved rattles clacked,
  as the shell hoops spoke to the ritual sticks.
  Once there was a silence; no one stirred; I heard my heart beat.
  Then, like an arrow's thud, one beat of a drum, one . . .
  another . . . another . . . a fourth—

and suddenly all the drums were thunder
and everyone leaped singing and surging in the last dance . . .
That was my first potlatch . . .

LEG—Ah but what about your father?   Your picture's far too gay.
He'd have nothing but a hangover and a smell of fish next day.

CHIEF—In those times we drank only our sounds and thoughts,
giving unhurt to those who gave.
When your fathers took our food and left us little coins,
when they took our songs and left us little hymns,
the music and the potlatch stopped.

LEG—And a good thing, Chief.   Really, now do you suppose
That we'd go back to living with a fishbone through our nose?

CHIEF—That was the Nootka Salish.
Our women were content, like yours,
to dangle copper from their ears
and paint their faces for the Winter Dance Moon.

LEG—Touché, my friend—but you're not going to say
That people lived in comfort on the Inlet in your day.
No nylon, solar heating, no modern way of life,
No jet planes, telephones or t.v., no gadgets for the wife—

CHIEF—Comfort is peace.

LEG—Eh?

CHIEF—Comfort was in the dogwool suit of my youth,
the tassels of flying squirrel
tailing like smoke from my shoulders,
not the trader's cast-offs in my aging.
Comfort was the winter's bear-haunches safe in the rafters,
when as a child I darted laughing under the reed hangings,
with a little fist of hazelnuts clutched from the cedar chest.
Comfort was waking beside my wife
on our bed of musk-sweet rushes.

19

LEG—I give up.   You're full of moonshine and romance.
> You've never learned the meaning of that great word "advance."
> Yet you lived till 1850—did you never realize
> What it meant to build this nation, to grow up, to civilize?

CHIEF—Before even the Captain's cloud-canoe, before I was chief,
> the Sechelts held a great gift-giving on the tiderim.
> Something, flung gleaming through the air, fell in the water.
> I dived; my fingers clutched a gun, a flintlock.
> Spaniards had made it;
> the Nootkas gave its height in otter skins.
> Now it was mine; I shot the deer my arrows fainted to reach.
> With other years came other traders
> and stronger fire unsealed from iron tube and bottle;
> I gave my only son the flintlock.
> He walked into the whiskey-house they built in our village;
> he drank its madness;
> he killed his cousin, my brother's heir.
> The white men choked my son with a rope.
> From that day my life was a walking backwards.

LEG—Well, such things happened, let's admit,
> But it's not like that today.
> We dont let Indians drink so much, it doesnt really pay.
> And let's be fair: without the white
> You never would have learned
> To read and write, hold down a job,
> Get paid for what you earned.

CHIEF—What trails we would have stumbled on alone none now will
> know.
> In a moon of heat the tall priest came;
> with his magic twig of fire he lit the dried grass
> and spoke in the raven's voice of Hell,
> unrolled a painting bright as the sundown,
> showed us our dead in Hell's flame.

In fear we let the little wisps of our marvels
lose themselves in the black cloud of his god.
And ever the whites came crowding our shoreline
like summer smelts, and the deer fled.
My grandsons, my hunters, went to grease logs for the skidders;
one died under a felled tree,
the other black and gasping with smallpox.

LEG—White men's diseases; sure, it's all very sad;
    But lots of you lived; it couldnt have been so bad.

CHIEF—I had yet two daughters; their eyes were chaste.
To one a sailor gave rum, and a glass necklace,
and the secret rot of his thighs; she died barren and young.
The other went to be squaw to a trader;
when he had turned her away,
before she spat out her lungs with his plague,
she bore him my only grand-daughter.
In my old age the child grew tall, fair as a waterfall.
The factor married her; he made her give up our people.
There are white chiefs now in Vancouver who carry her blood,
but it is a long time now and they do not know,
or they are ashamed.
These are all my descendants . . .

LEG—Hmm.  Well.  I've no more questions.

MIN—Mr. Powers?

POW—Old Chief and challenge, toll us your own end.

CHIEF—When the measles passed from my village, ten of us lived
to bury our ninety, and I, their Chief, was blind.
We left the longhouses for the burning,
the burial grove and the carvings to loggers.
They sent me over the Sound to sit
dark and alone by the smokehouse fire of my cousins.
One night I felt with shuffling feet the beach-path.
I walked into the saltwater,
I walked down to the home of the Seal Brother . . .

MIN— . . . Thank you, Chief . . . Are there any more questions?

LEG—No.

POW—Your doom's long paid, o hewed man. The questions come to those who chief and cheaply bought it.

MIN—Farewell, Chief.

CLERK—Please de-materialize this way, Chief.

CHIEF—(*Fading*) Peace to my cousins, comfort, and peace . . .

—— —— ——

POW—From the ash of the fir springs the fire-weed;
from the ask of his faring your fear.
His village died O not alone that Legion's might
more lofty lift, but so you could be meek to understay
your own swift Inding.

LEG—You think because we built Vancouver on his campsite
We're going to let you knock it down?
Give up our global future for a damsite?
Come off! We've just begun to build this town.

POW—What would you do with time but teem?

LEG—Why everything! You wait and see. Someday we'll be
The universe's capital, the solar super-city.
It took two billion years to get things ready for us.
We want another billion in the kitty.

POW—My Office is not prepared to ante more than five.

LEG—Five! Five years? Mr. Minister, I brought a witness—
A geologist—O, yes, I know, he's technically alive;
But he's been waiting all this time in hope to testify.
Will you consent? He'll show we need more years than five!

MIN—Who is he?

LEG—Professor Seen, sir, from the U.B.C. A scientist—impartial.
He lives *outside* the city in the lowest-rental housing;
No vote, investment, bank account; no boosting and no grousing.

MIN—I think, Mr. Powers, we might count him one of the dead for our
   purposes? Any objections if we let the rule slide this once?

Pow—Sliderule or transit, all geo-logic works for me. Agreed.

MIN—Call Professor Seen from the ante-room.

CLERK—Perfesser Seen . . . Perfesser Seen.

PROF— . . . Coming . . . Here, gentlemen.

CLERK—Full name?

PROF—Seen, S-E-E-N, Edward Oscar, E. O. Seen.

MIN—Sorry to have kept you waiting, Professor. Your witness, Mr.
   Legion.

LEG—Would you please, professor, tell us first the story
         Of how Vancouver's area was created,
      How long a time it took to shape this wondrous human home
         That powerful Interests want annihilated?

Pow—Or interested Powers.

PROF—From planet's birth      two billion years perhaps
        till these shores shook,     roared shuddering,
        flat coast cracked,       cast up its granite,
        hurled lava fuming       four miles high
        built batholiths      from Burrard to the Yukon.

LEG—And then?

PROF—Sixty millions more      for mountains to chill,
        grow soil-skin,      suffer valleys,
        till warping from palms      went the winged lizards.
        Hundred-foot horsetails       the horny ones trampled,
        tyrannosaurs crashed      like cold kangaroos.

LEG—That's two billion, sixty million.

PROF—Twenty million years      for such monsters to pass
        while southwards volcanoes      seethed to the sky-vault and
        sly cat-mammals      swelled into sabre-tooths.

LEG—Two billion and eighty.

23

PROF—And then a mere       half-million summers
    as slowly clouds thicken,     airs cool, falls the snow.
    Magnolias under     the ice-mounds moulder,
    and south move the hairy ones,     mammoth and mastodon.

LEG—And Vancouver?

PROF—Here incubus ice     arcs over all,
    presses the shore's bones     into the seabed,
    licks out fjords,     levels the lean peaks
    and glittering, humps over     the globe's round head.
    Melts then, lingering back,     leaving heaped moraines,
    letting land rise,     birds from the lean trees sing.
    Yet thrice inches forward,     thrice falls away from us.
    Since last it pulsed back     to poise at the Pole
    count twenty milleniums,     thirty it may be,
    for firs to flourish     and deer to find them,
    for berries and bears,     partridge in bracken.

LEG—Two billion, eighty million, five hundred and thirty thousand
    years. Gentlemen, you see! And not even man yet! Tell us,
    Professor, how long since man?

PROF—Since brown longheads     leaped across Bering
    slid down these coasts     spearing the salmon
    hardly two hundred     centuries have hovered.
    Man, sir, this morning     moved down to visit.

LEG—Thank you, Doctor; thank you, Professor.
    You've heard the truth, the truth, God bless her.
    Two billion years and more this Eden was a-borning,
    But Eve and I found it only this morning.
    Now is there anyone, Socred or Tory,
    Who wants this Paradise blown to glory?
    Mr. Powers he's your witness. Thank you, Professor!

POW—Man-Cain this brief dove-mourning-morning came
    and when a-wither by your paleologic clocks?
    O sage promessor, say.

PROF—Before the sun sets       silence returns.
    After a thousand       generations the glacier,
    icecap again,       earthpress and frost,
    or earlier even       eruption and lava flow.
    Later may limp back       life of some sort,
    empire renewed       by insect or rat,
    till sun overswell—

POW—And then?

PROF—          Then sand is world
    and seas steaming      under the stars.

POW—And no escape?

PROF—Though life leap to Mars      it is lost in this fury.

POW—And then?

PROF—What Sun brings after      is Sun's business only.

POW—You hear.   To blow this vain Mancover skywards now
    is to advanquish by a jingle comic second
    what Adamizing Father Sun once planned.

MIN—No more questions?

POW—No, and thank you, Prophetic-facer Sane.

MIN—Mr. Legion?

LEG—No!

MIN—Thank you, Professor Seen.   You may retire.

CLERK—Will Perfesser Seen please de-materialize this way.

PROF—But—

MIN—Wait!   Dont do that!   He's still alive!

CLERK—O, sorry sir.   Just step along, perfesser.

PROF—Thank you.   Goodbye, gentlemen . . .

———      ———      ———

MIN—Who's next, Mr. Legion?   I fancy you're willing to try the dead
   again?   Shall I suggest—?

LEG—No. No more Indians.  I'll pick my own.
Someone who knew Vancouver from away back.
With your permission, Mr. Minister, I'm calling up
A Mr. J. C. Deighton, known as Gassy Jack.

MIN—Gassy Jack!  Old Gastown's pioneering barkeep?

LEG—Vancouver's first guest-lodge proprietor,
A real old-timer, and a founding-father.

POW—A rye and risky choice, Mr. Allegiance.

MIN—You'll have to watch his language, Mr. Legion.  We're on the air you know.  Call up Mr. Jack Deighton.

CLERK—Mr. J. C. Deighton, Mr. J. C. Deighton,
Materialize this way, please.

JACK— . . . Ahoy! . . . At your service, gents.  What'll it be?

LEG—You are Mr. J. C. Deighton, proprietor of the Deighton Arms, in the settlement of Granville, later incorporated as the City of Vancouver?

JACK—Granville?  Come off it, mate.  That was the nobs' name. Some politician puttin in his horns.  Gastown it was really called. *You* know that.  Recorded in the Admiralty charts.  Named after me, no less, after Gassy Jack, the greatest talker west of Hull. That's where I was born, in old England, and a Hull of a place too, if you gents dont mind an old sailor—

MIN—I'm afraid some of our audience may, Mr. Deighton.  You'll have to keep it clean if you want to stay materialized.

JACK—Cor love a duck, now all I was sayin was how Vancouver was really called Gastown, all because of me and so you ought to know how I come to be Gassy Jack—

MIN—I think we've got that point—

JACK—It was because I was born in Hull on a howlin November night, one of them North Sea Roarers like, and I'd no sooner opened me lug to yell for air than I caught enough sea-wind to toot me horn the rest of me nateral life.  (*Laughs*)  Not that it wernt a kind of

26

unnateral life, really, you might say I had, havin run away to sea
before me mother could say lor-lumme—

LEG—Very interesting, Jack, and now tell us, what do you think of
Vancouver today?

JACK—Vancouver? Today? Cor, it's a sight aint it? Like Hull all
over again, a bit. You know what? You know, when I first seen
it, it wernt nothin but a tincan sawmill and a bunch of floatshacks?
Dont know how I stuck it, me wot had once been bosn's mate on a
clipper ship, servin out belayin-pin soup to jollies, and roamin the
seven soggy seas. But I ad to stick it, of course; all me gear was
three barrels of whiskey, me old yaller bulldog and two cluckin
hens. And me old squaw, of course.

LEG—Yes, yes, Jack, those were the days. But now it's different eh?
What do you think of us now?

JACK—Ah, ye got hotels bigger nor icebergs now, mate, but they're
as cold to the soul, man. What can ye drink in em but wish-
washy beer and not a smidgeon of grub to clamp it. It's all like
a Methodist wake, with never a song or a salt water tale. The old
Deighton Arms, ah, now that was the hub of the port, so to speak;
the loggers' opry house and the town theayter. And if a sailor
wanted the news or a tall story, there was me, Gassy Jack, to—

MIN—The witness must stick to the point. Mr. Legion only wants to
know whether you approve of Vancouver today, in general.

JACK—Ay, sorry, Capn, but you know how it is with an old seadog.
Vancouver, eh? Well, it's a lubberly big place for sure, aint it
now? Though the loggers aint changed much, the old sons of
bachelors, still leapin at each others faces on the skid road with
their great calked boots the way they used to in the Deighton Arms.
What a time I ad with 'em. But the sailors aint wot they used to
be. A bunch of scowmen now they are. Why, when I—

LEG—Yes, yes. But times change, Jack, and you were one of those
who started changing them. Doesnt it make you proud to see the
result?

JACK—O, ay; howsoever I'd like it better if they adnt changed the name. They waited till I'd turned up me toes, you know. It was them land sharks did it. And hearken, ye know twas only a month atter, the whole kaboodle burned down, and the Deighton Arms with it? One of them landshark's stump fires got away, it was, rattle their teeth! It's all new, this Vancouver you got, and to tell you the truth, mates, I wouldnt stick 'ere now; it's the Artic I'd head for if I was young and alive. Take Aklavik; I hear the Eskymoes have the family allowance checks and drink their wiskey neat; now may be the Mounties up there wouldnt be too hard on a honest saloon-keeper and a sailor with a hundred yarns in his head—

LEG—Man, man, if it's money you want, Vancouver's where they make it. This is no bleak outpost we're talking about now but a great fine prosperous city. And the point is, there are those who want to get rid of it, let it go back to the woods and the Indians. What do you think of that?

JACK—Twould be a waste, no doubt; though now you speak of it, I allus had a soft spot for the klootch girls. I'd a kept shipshape if me old squaw had lived, the one I got up the Fraser when I was steamboatman, duckin the bullets her tribe popped from the bushes every time I ran the shoals past their village; for I heaved her away so fast I kind of forgot to pay the chief for her, you know. That was atter me and Kennedy gave up pannin the mud to Till's Bar and beyond, washin after the Yankee desperadoes, for they'd whipped away all the nuggets ahead of us. (You fellows know all about that—they're still doin it to you.) She was a good squaw though and she run me first tavern neat as a quarterdeck, the Globe Saloon in New Westminster that was, mates—run it till the wiskey dismasted me and I went up to Douglas Springs for a cure—I'd a hogshead mouth in them days. Trouble was I fetched her along and left me bar to a Yankee to care for, one that sailed with me in the old Invincible. Come the Fourth of July that son of a soaked sea-biscuit got himself soused and served out free every last peg of

me wiskey, blew all me cash on firecrackers, and shipped hisself off
to Frisco.   By the time I was back, two other saloons was up and had
all the trade.   If it wernt that me squaw had forty silver dollars
stowed away under the outhouse, we'd a never been able to buy
them three barrels of wiskey and move to the Inlet, and there never
would a been Gastown at all, my jollies.

LEG—Very interesting, Jack, but let's get back—

JACK—Two barrels with a plank over em and one barrel on top, that
was all we started with, and a belayin pin off the old Invincible to
settle the fights.   And a license old Kennedy got me, bless me old
shipmate.   But it was me squaw kept us goin, and when the money
come pourin in (for the Customs Johnny had took to his bed with
rheumatics, and the Frisco skippers rolled the hogsheads off to me
like any Free Port), it was me old squaw built most of the Deighton
Arms, with a sailor or two had skipped ship and was workin for rum.
But then, mates, she up and died on me, quick like, just from a bit
of mumps she come afoul of and I was a stoven man from then on.
For I sent out to Hull and paid passage for a pair of me nephews.
And a set of limey lily-livers they were, by the great anchor, would
lie awake afeerd for their skins when they heard the deer at night
clompin over the board-walk behind the saloon.   In a month they
left me.   They were great blabbermouths too and in no time at all
there was a Sydney duck had a saloon only three stumps away,
and that brought the river police sniffin and a new Customs Johnny
and there was duty to pay on every noggin.   So when me relatives
skipped I got me a new squaw, a soncy young lass she was.   And
though I had to pay the old Chief high for her an she'd go on a tear
every month and sell up the furniture (when I was out on a spree)
and scuttle back to the tribe, and I'd have to fetch her again, howsoever she was a round warm klootch and a worker, and if it's all the
same to you gen'mn, I'd be glad if you called her up and let the two
of us nip out for a tot when you're through with me here.

MIN—Just a minute! Just a minute Mr. Deighton! You've been materialized solely to answer questions at this hearing. And then you go back to—wherever you were.

JACK—Aye, aye Cap'n. I would like a wet of the whistle, though. Did I tell ye—?

MIN—And now please, Mr. Legion, keep your witness to the subject.

LEG—I'll try sir. Look, Jack, we havent much more time. All we want to know is do you, as a pioneer citizen of Van—of Gastown, do you approve of the proposal to end it, blow it up, or whatever they're going to do to it?

JACK—Blood! Blow it up? That's a violent thought, that is. I never was one for violence. You take fights in saloons, frinstance, always somethin broken, head or a bottle. Not good for business it aint. Not that I aint seen plenty of rough stuff, as you can imagine, mates. Why I was all up the Cariboo Trail, dodgin hordes of grizzlies and Yankee roadagents and greaser bandits, and shootin rapids big as North Sea breakers. And before that I was in Callyforny, at the Feather River diggins. That was the place! Would you believe it, genmn, I hadnt been there two weeks when I washed a ten thousand dollar nugget, big as a galley-mug. Ah, and it was violence done me out of it, violence and Yankee trickery, mates. For I had two pardners, see, and we all dealt a round of stud to see who'd take it to Frisco and bring back the cash, and I won with three Queens. But on the ferry I met an old deckswabber from Hull and a slick kind of matey of his from the East. And they had in their tow a wench from Mexico way. Well, mates, what with the old tar's rum, and the black eyes of that senorita, and the smooth palaver that Yankee put over, all I had left for the nugget next mornin was a dried nigger's head (twas a souvenir from the Fiji), a yaller bullpup and the Mexican wench. And when I brought them all back to me pardners, one of em bonked me on the crown with the black man's skull, and t'other made off with the senorita. They'd have heaved me into the Feather River if it hadnt of been

30

the bullpup was all on my side and took to sampling their shins.
As it was they run the pup and me out of the diggins and that's
how I come to the Fraser and—

LEG—Please! We're talking about *now*, Vancouver, the fate of a city!

MIN—If the witness has no more than this to tell us, we must de-
materialize him at once.

JACK—No, wait. Forgive an old sailor. Gassy by name, gassy by
nature. There *is* somethin I'd like to say to you gents, if I can
get me tongue around it. Mr. Legion here, he's worried about his
city. Somebody's plannin to get rid of it. How, I dunno; another
fire mebbe, a big shootin match, it don't matter. The point he's
trying to make is it shouldnt happen nohow. But it seems to me,
why all the worry? Big ports, why they're a dime a dozen; when
a sailor's young, a port's a place to get drunk and make love in,
and then to set sail out of, fast. When he's old and tired of the
sea, what he wants is a place like old Gastown, a place that's, well,
small, with clean water around it yet, and great thumpin trees,
and deer wanderin in at night. Or even supposin he's set on a city,
it dont have to be Vancouver. There's plenty of others. Course,
as I say, I dont like violence. Supposin now you get Mr. Powers
to agree to move all your friends out, the folks you want to keep,
scatter em up the coast maybe, startin new places? You and him
splice hands on it. And let the rest go down to Davy Jones.

Pow—O Judgment Deighton, whom would you sheep from goats?

JACK—If it were me I'd jest ship out the pretty girls (them that work
spry and help a man), and the folk that really laugh and have fun;
the rest dont matter. There's an awful lot of hippycrites in cities,
you know, mates—cardsharps and slick traders and landsharks
and psalm-singers. I never liked most preachers, for example; and
it puts me in mind of a story. You genm'n ever hear the one about
the missionary and the bosn's girl? Seems they were shipwrecked
together, see, and—

LEG—Please, Jack, not here—

JACK—When it come night-time—

MIN—Clerk, de-materialize the witness at once.

CLERK—Mr. J. C. Deighton.  Please de-materialize this way at once!

JACK—(*Fading*): Avast there!  Wait!  You aint heard the rest of me story . . .

POW—There goes the very gas the city swelled from.

MIN—I'm sorry, gentlemen, but we couldnt risk him any longer.

LEG—It's all your fault, consistently refusing
　　　Any witness of my choosing.
　　　I'm through with all this legal fooling.
　　　I'm registering an appeal against your ruling.

MIN—But I havent ruled yet, Mr. Legion, you know.

POW—My worried friend forgets old Gusty Jack was his own wittyness.

LEG—Well, the Minister wouldnt let him stay.

MIN—You want him back?

LEG—No!  Nor any other.

MIN—Very well.  Mr. Powers, your Office may now bring forward any relevant testimony.

———————　　———————　　———————

POW—The Offence of the Future, Mr. Minister, presumpts one whitness from the past, and he'll consent us.

MIN—His name?

POW—Long Will.

MIN—Long Will what?

POW—Mayhap of Langland or the Malvern Hills.

LEG—Never heard of him.

POW—He lived no less, my learning friend, and with his poet's hand plucked London's praying pride six sanctuaries agone.  May he be culled?

MIN—Call Long Will of Langland—the author, I believe, of *Piers the Plowman?*

Pow—Right, sir.

CLERK—(*Calling*) Long Will of Land—the author of-I-believe—what
was that, sir?

MIN—*Piers* (or *Peter*) *the Plowman*, a poem of Chaucer's time—but
never mind. Long Will of Langland is enough.

CLERK—Long Will of Langland, please materialize this way.

LANG— . . . God save you sirs, and grace us all.

MIN—Welcome, Long Will.

LEG—I really must object, sir, to hauling in this witness.
How could he know Vancouver? I challenge here his fitness.

Pow—He walks her streets and straits unseen each day.

LEG—A medieval long-hair, a foreigner, another of these queers.
And the government admits that he's been dead six hundred years.

MIN—It's my impression, Mr. Legion, that the author of *Piers Plowman*
enjoys a form of life as potent as, let us say, Mr. Deighton's.
Objection over-ruled. You may proceed with your witness, Mr.
Powers.

Pow—Tell us, Long While, what see you in Vinecouver? What saw
you, say, this yesterday?

LANG—Yester? Yester in the morning I mused on Little Mountain
saw a city wake and wink its million windows.
Squared it lay, squamous with shingle and cement,
straitly ruled by steel, by stark wire and stucco.
South walked a hoary wood-waste of houses
massing to the river like lemmings on the march,
jerry-new cottages jostling jowl by jowl
(except to skirt green fields golfers locked away)
down to the fouled and profit-clogged Fraser,
the pile-impaled river plotting its flood.
Then I saw hurrying a horde from this honeycomb,
clever carls and feckless, men fair and swart,
millhands and waitresses out to work and wonder,

33

> bakers, butchers, and brewsters many,
> and veterans of vain wars or wars soon to be.
> I saw them tramp hard streets straight as their faces,
> huddle into busses and hurry down to jail.
> Then I looked east—

Leg—Mr. Minister, I must again object.
> This is a most unfair account,
> A dreary flim-flam full of dialect,
> And not a word about the things that count.

Pow—All the biter for you, Mr. Allegion, when you come to crass-examine.

Leg—But I can see he's just begun;
> Please let me get one word in—one!

Min—Perhaps, Mr. Powers, you wouldnt mind if Mr. Legion were occasionally to interrupt the witness with questions?

Pow—Neither object nor objections to the quest or to the questions.

Leg—All right then, just to start with,
> Does this witness realize
> When he runs down our metropolis
> How fast it got to be this size?
> Seventy years ago a tent-town,
> Rock and bush and stump,
> Mud for sidewalks, cows for tractors,
> Just a loggers' dump.
> Now—almost two million people!
> And our river, Mr. Long Will,
> May be dirty—but it's *busy:*
> Every quarter-mile a mill;
> Last year we got another
> Billion dollars out of trees;
> And there's salmon in that Fraser—
> Twenty million bucks from these,
> Then there's—

34

LANG—Yea, all this yammer I hear, yet it yieldeth me naught.

LEG—Yah, yammer yourself! You—

MIN—Please, Mr. Legion.

LEG—Well, look—he didnt even mention
    Our modern civic jetport, or the Plasticville Extension.

LANG—I saw the Seven Sinners soaring from your airports,
    heading up in haste to overhaul the honest,
    to comb at will the prone land, the long comely nation,
    that n'er is long nor fair enough to end their lust for rifling.
    Then I looked eastward, saw a legion more
    of harried eyes hurrying down the hill for wages,
    makers of brassieres, business cards and bowling pins,
    mild folk or merciless, maidens clean and clabbered.
    But, as the sun charmed them, children came halooing,
    their eyes still alight from all the wine of living,
    skirmishing off to schoolrooms under bright skies.
    Yet many learned only with machines to mesh themselves,
    more to win for the self than to work for the world's good.
    West then my eyes turned—

LEG—West so soon! Saw you nought else in the east? O damn, now
    he's got me doing it!
    Look, Mr. Will, our workers arent dejected—
    They've got the highest standards in the universe—
    (Americans, of course, are always excepted)—
    And if they couldnt work they'd feel a lot worse.
    They've got frigidaires—gas furnaces—and a twelve hour week.
    You ought to think twice before you speak.
    And sneering at BC's Progressive Education!
    Why in workshop equipment we lead the whole nation.

MIN—Was that a question, Mr. Legion?

LEG—No.

Pow—Please continue, Mr. Longlast.  You were about to descry the
wastern view.

Lang—Yea, then I moved west to my hill's margin
and saw a soft middleclass swaddled in trees,
in unfrequented churches and fears not a few.
Chained as fast to profits as poorer folk to wages,
roofs and hopes high, yet higher still their mortgages.
Some knew nobleness and neighbourly lived;
some had milk in morning to melt their belly's ulcers
and rode alone to office, an ego to an auto.

Leg—Mr. Minister, to listen to this witness
I challenge the wisdom—
He's attacking Christianity and
The whole profit system.

Pow—All the batter for your case, Mr. 'Ligion, if my wetness prove
submersive.

Leg—But he's talking like a red—at a Public Hearing!

Pow—My wordly friend need not be up-armed.  Master Langland is
colour-deaf and treats this merely as a Public Seeing.

Min—Is Mr. Powers regretting that he gave Mr. Legion leave to
interrupt?

Pow—No, sir.  I should be gleed if Mr. Legion inter-raps whenever he
lacks.

Leg—I'll take you at your word, whatever it is.

Min—Now, let Mr. Long Will get on with his.

Pow—Mr. Alackland?  North now?

Lang—Yea, north I gazed last, through a skyfull of grime,
glimpsed the grizzled harbours and a graveyard of smokestacks,
a wilderness of wires and a weedbed of poles.

Leg—Bosh!  Our climate's wonderful all the year through,
But you cant have industry and keep your sky blue.

LANG—Beyond the tamed shores that no tide cleansed
      rose the raped mountains scarred with fire and finance
      and raddled with the lonely roofs of the rich,
      of barristers and bookies and brokers aplenty,
      of agents for septic tanks, aspirin or souls.
      Executives, crooners, con-men a few,
      union-chiefs, generals, and advertising counsellors,
      dowagers and doctors and dealers in froth.

LEG—Now look—some rich are maybe crooked, but most of them are
      straight,
      And you're talking of the houses of folk who really rate,
      Homes like Old England's or homes of tomorrow—
      What do you mean they're lonely?   And where's all this sorrow?
      Gardens full of roses, their own private creeks,
      All nestling at the foot of the snowcapped peaks.

MIN—We've been very patient, Mr. Legion, but I must insist, if you're
    going to continue interrupting the witness, you find more interesting
    clichés than 'snowcapped peaks' . . . Go on Mr. Langland.

LANG—Down I strayed then as the sun stood above me,
      past surgeons assembling to save saint and gangster,
      trod down Cambie to the tall grey town.
      Heard from presses plashing the papers of the eunuchs
      mopping up each morning great Money's harem
      and piping facts falsetto for fear of burly Truth.
      Heard the haste of Hastings and the howl of an ambulance,
      and the sibilants where thousands thronged in a slum
      with little skill to leave it, since their skins were yellow.

LEG—Picturesque Chinatown, with its night life and fun,
      Chow main, and curios—he calls it a slum!

MIN—Please, Mr. Legion.

LANG—There were white slums too for I sniffed all their gaping,
      and the breaths of their babies souring as they grew.
      I gulped in gas as well and grey smog a lungfull.

Softly in Powell Street I heard the pimp's whisper,
heard the artful panting of the poxed prostitute.
Cordova Street was lined with loggers and 'leggers,
folk selling faith, firearms and cathartics,
honest men and reefers, rubadubs and bums—

LEG—Why I thought the skid-road boys would have been your chums—

LANG—Yea they hungered, or harried, while near enough in Howe Street
    unsought thieves wolfed thick steaks at luncheons—

LEG—Only a commie would make fun of service clubs.
    You ought—

LANG—I loped then to a harbour where high ships lay,
    and fish-heads floated in the fetid waters;
    saw longshoreman sweating and sailors aplenty
    while a shipload of salesmen sailed to a convention
    whiskeyed for the weekend and their wenches after.
    Then I drew to Granville, past drugs and deodorants,
    palaces for strip-tease, slot-machines and pool—

LEG—Is that all you saw in the gateway to the Orient?
    What about the world's most majestic liners?
    The yachts?   The romantic moonlight cruising
    And the special trips for visiting Shriners?

LANG—Blaring off to Bowen for a night of boozing.

LEG—Why that island's a fairyland of sylvan beauties—

LANG—A haven lined with hotdogs and hardeyed cuties.

LEG—A picknicker's paradise, the artists' haunt—

LANG—Yet they wander faint there to fill the soul's want.

LEG—You didnt look—

LANG—All such I marked but made of them no argument
    and strode then in Granville Street, as I said ere,
    my ears dinged with dollars, and cripples crying dire news.
    Saw poets dreaming slogans, painters peddling beer,
    laughing folk and louring, lightfoot and lame,

   stores full of sweating wives, weary clerks and trash,
   machine-turned totem poles, chewing-gum and time-clocks,
   and counters hung with lithographs of long ladies' thighs.

LEG—Whew! Wait a min—

LANG—Some books there were for thinking but many more to block it,
   Bibles for gunmen and great sheets for gamblers.

LEG—What a tourist you'd make! Dont you know Canadian shops
   Are full of the finest goods, the best Scottish wool,
   Linen from Belfast, and English bone chinas,
   Specially priced for American diners?

LANG—Down in pale alerooms democrats dawdled,
   mazed dark in movies or dreamed on the corners
   while wardheelers rode to polls to wangle the taxes,
   to money-change the Council and amend Magna Charta,
   and fat lawyers grappled in long lovers' clinches.

LEG—I wish you'd hang around Toronto for a change!

LANG—There—and here— I fared through streets of fallow faces,
   hearts that hop to hope or hate in tune with the headlines,
   mouths that curse His race today and roar Christ on Sunday.

LEG—There he is again, running down religion.

LANG—Came at last in twilight to a tree-tall park
   where ladies gawked through cages at their naked cousins
   or bared themselves on beaches that breathed of flesh and
    sewage—

LEG—Is this Stanley Park? ! Really Mr. Minister,
   The motives of this witness must certainly be sinister.
   Virginal timber—four thousand acres—
   Natural beaches (protected from breakers),
   Picnic grounds and totem poles,
   A giant pool and the Malkin Bowl!
   The dancer's mecca, the boater's dream,
   Alpine vistas, and tea with cream.

Why this is where our city folks release all their tensions!
And even a hellfire preacher might mention
The coloured fountain in Lost Lagoon or
The special canoes for the honeymooner.

LANG—Yea, when I walked under boughs away from the bathers
I marked how the lovers moved from the moon's eye
for love is illegal and laid away in bushes.

LEG—Ah! Free love now!

LANG—Nay, but lacking love, all this living's lifeless,
love, too, of truth, and for our children's children,
joy in giving joy, and gaining love by loving,
lust of peace and fair thoughts, and loyalty to man.
Though many walk fat and proud thy folk are sick with fear,
taking the time's toys and trashing all the future,
lunatic in laughter, lost in mere getting,
and haunted by a skydoom their own hates have dealt . . .

POW—Thank you, Master Wail. Your wightness, Mr. Legion.

LEG—Well all I need to say is, we've got faith in B. C.
Our motto's "We Prosper By Land and By Sea."
There's billions still to be made from our greenery
And the mountains will always be there for scenery.
We're the hub of Tomorrow, the Future's baby,
We're here to stay, and I dont mean maybe.

POW—Excuse me, Mr. Minister, but on a point of infamation, my louded friend is massinformed. He states Wancouver is the Future's baby, but my Office nowhen admits paternity. The Past, sir, we contend, alone is putative.

MIN—The point's well taken . . . Has your witness finished?

LANG—Yea.

POW—He's finite, sir, and fain to vanish unless my lurid friend would care to Christian him further.

LEG—That one-day tourist? He doesnt know the score.
He's a medieval Bolshevik—I've had enough and more.

40

MIN—Thank you then, Mr. Langland, and good-day.

CLERK—Mr. Langland, please de-materialize this way.

LANG (*Fading*): Good day and God save ye, God save ye all . . .

———    ———    ———

MIN—Well, gentlemen, there seem to be no more witnesses, nor further reasons for continuing this hearing. Have you any comments at this time, Mr. Powers?

POW—A comma only, to the sentence each witness has pronounced. The Future here contends, sir, no reason has been rhymed why we should not proceed to damn.

MIN—Very well. Anything to add, Mr. Legion?

WOMAN—Just a minute, Mr. Minister.

MIN—What? Who's that?

WOMAN—This is a Public Hearing, sir?

MIN—Why, yes, but who are you?

WOM—A public hearer. I live just two blocks east.

MIN—But havent you a TV set, a radio at least?

WOM—I turned it off and came to testify.

MIN—But if you've listened you'll know the reason why—

WOM—I cant be heard? Because I live and love
and hate? We'll see. You, Mr. Powers,
if you are really Powers and sit above,
you cannot fear what a mere living housewife says?

POW—My unpliant clients neither fear nor favour, madam. Stay saying on for all your hours.

WOM—And you, Mr. Legion, though I'm no civic notable you've in-
invited,
And we have thoughts as far apart as moon and sun,
And though I grant each ill these ghosts today have cited—
Yet gladly do I walk beneath this city's sky and will till I'm
undone.

41

LEG—You mean you *like* Vancouver?   At last someone to tell the truth!
    I'd come to think that I was nuts.
    Of course we want to have your testimony, lady,
    Now, Mr. Minister, *please*, no ifs or buts.

MIN—It's as you wish, though since she seems to be alive, her testimony
    cant go in the record.

CLERK—Name, please.

WOM—My name is Anyone's.

STEN—How do you spell—?

CLERK—Mrs. N. E. Wuns.   W-U-N-S, I guess.   That right, madam?

WOM—Any way.

MIN—All right, madam.   But remember you're not in the record.

WOM—Whether the record mutes me
    Or my child unloose me to sorrow,
    Whether the glaciers glide
    Or the sun scream down tomorrow—
    I woke today with my husband
    To the bronze clashing of peaks,
    To the long shout of the ocean,
    And the blood alive in my cheeks.
    Though the jetplanes drew their chalklines
    Over my blackboard sky
    The eraser sun undid them
    And a mastering hawk walked high.
    Two flickers knocked on a cedar's door
    Three finch ran fugues through the wind
    And the scent of primula moved in my world
    However my world had sinned.

POW—O pettafull lady, is this all your shell and shelter from the blast?
    The Future hedonizes not these sinsualities
    And though your smile is dew upon a mourning web
    Our snake has Eved the spider.

WOM—And yet I live, damnation is not now.
        The hill of Paradise is always passed and hell lifts plain.
    These twain the sweet hard mountains of our purgatory
      Our will has raised and will again.

LEG—Madam, go on, that's good, dont let him bother you.
    If you need help, I'll father you.

WOM—I am the cool Vancouver's kin, not yours
      And fosterdaughter to that Headman mild;
    In the professor's logic I am woven,
    By the rank sailor's flesh my mind is cloven
      And I am yet the priestly plowman's child.
    For all mankind is matted so within me
      Despair can find no earthroom tall to grow;
    My veins run warm however veers time's weather;
      I breathe Perhaps and May and never No.
    Under the cool geyser of the dogwood
      Time lets me open books and live;
    Under the glittering comment of the planets
      Life asks, and I am made to give.

POW—Perhappy child, there's still the wrackening.
    For every favour fever, for any joy a jail.
    Pompeian ladies loved the outlean of Vesuvius.

WOM—Because of the machine in us we toil in blankness,
    Because of the green bulb is us we leaf to joy.
    The mortal cells divide to pain, to laughter,
    Whether the horse is brought to Point Grey or to Troy.

LEG—Now, maam, dont let him put you off the track.
    I'd like to have you tell the Minister
    Something about our climate, and our factories,
    And all the sights from Bowen to Westminster!

WOM—I'm not your witness.   I need your silence only.

Leg—Why listen, lady, you're practically a poet, I can see.
  If you can keep this up and cover all the region
  We'll have the Tourist Bureau print a million copies
  They'll never damn us then or my name isnt Legion.

Wom—Your name is not Legion—mine is.

Leg—Now wait a min—

Wom—And only in your absence can I speak.

Leg—Mr. Minister, I protest. I—

Min—Really, madam, you must—

Wom—Clerk, de-materialize this gentleman, this living ghost.

Clerk—(*Automatically*): Will Mr. Legion please de-materialize this way.

Leg—Hey wait! You cant do this to me!

Min—Hold on! I'm still presiding here.

Wom—Presiding, but you cannot interfere. You're only history . . .
  Come Mr. Pseudo-Legion, be gone, be ghosted.

Leg—Wait! I still have to summarize my case! I protest!
  I aint (*Fading*) dead, it isnt fair, I'm still alive . . . alive . . .
  alie . . .

Min—Well . . . must confess I've wanted to do that myself for a
  long time. However, young lady, it's very irregular conduct on
  your part; hmmn . . . high time I closed this Hearing.

Wom—I've more to say to Mr. Powers, but the rest of you may go if
  you wish. We'll lock up. Clerk, give me the key, please.

Clerk—Right, ma'am, thank you . . . Catch.

Wom—Oops! . . . Got it.

Min—Now, now, not *quite* so fast. First I must declare the Hearing
  ended, you know. Then there's my judgment. Judgment is, of
  course—

Pow—Suspended!

Min—Naturally. Now—let's shut off the television—Where's that
  Announcer?

44

CLERK—Beg, pardon, sir, he stopped telecasting some time ago and went home—it was when Gassy Jack came on.

MIN—He did? Hmmm. And what about the tape recording, Miss Take?

STEN—I'm sorry, sir; that broke a long way back, when Mr. Legion was shouting at Mr. Powers.

MIN—Dear, dear. You have your own notes, of course?

STEN—Just what I could spell, sir . . . May I go now?

MIN—I guess so. Hmmm . . . I suppose we'd better all go. Coming, Mr. Powers?

POW—Coming but nowhere gone. I stay enchantressed by our leading lady.

MIN—Well, it's your private hearing now, and no records taken. Come, Mr. Clerk, we've a job on our hands: the Missing Persons Bureau will want some kind of report on Legion.

CLERK—Yes, sir, in milluplicate, sir. (*Fading*) Good-night Mr. Powers, good-night ma'am.

STEN—(*Fading*): Nightie-nightie, everybody.

MIN—Night, Mr. Powers. Judgment reserved *sine die*. Good-night, madam. (*Fading*) Dont forget to lock up.

POW—God's night, Mr. Moonister, and a good waning . . .

   Madoom, my compliments. You guessed these ghost-men out. And now?

WOM—Now you.

POW—Me? Ho! I'm allwise just behind your reach—and yet I hold you.

WOM—But ever I am loosed by hope.

POW—And lost, in this unhopey world.

WOM—No. My mind's unconquered.

POW—Men conquer their own minds, and canker others'.

WOM—By all the past we know our freedom is renewable each moment.

45

Pow—By all your Past the Future has condoomed you.
    Prepare to follow Legion to the ghosts.

Wom—No!  Never!  I am mistress over you, My Master Powers—
    The only future's what I make each hour.

Pow—The Captain never wished his trees away for you
    And he and they are gone, and all discovery's dew.

Wom—Each day discovery delights me,
      My child's quick thought, old music newly heard;
    The friend emerging from the stranger lights me
      Along the ever-branching lanes of human search.

Pow—Lanes that straggle only to the sun's sahara.

Wom—Till sun sears we make him sire us.
    Till then all shapes and sounds will fire us,
    Our thinkers knit them and our artists net.

Pow—Think you in these to find the Headman's peace?
    That bard of paradays is plucked
    and all his comeforth gone beyond Vancovery.
    Your world is armagadding;
    no conjury of little folk undoes its warlocks.
    You're now too billion many.

Wom—The more to want and thus to will—and then we've caught it.
    How many leaps of light away peace spins
    My heart builds its long telescope to plot it.

Pow—But what is peace if all the earth's a gassy Jacktown?

Wom—It still has its becoming.
    There's not a day that kindness does not rise
    Like grass through every pavement's crack.

Pow—What?  Through every mastered Longlank strait?

Wom—His eyes were on the sins he loved to hate.
    He heard the bomb but not the children whistling.
    Yet children grown may sing a doom awry.

46

He did not stay to see the selfless deeds that multiply
And wander like simmering bees across my city's gardens,
Storing for winter all that summer pardons.

Pow—But lady, lady, I threaten everthelease.

Wom—How could I know, without the threat of death, I lived?

Pow—But do you know why you defy me?

Wom—That you might also be.
Without my longer Will, my stubborn boon,
You'd have no mate to check with but the cornered moon.
It's my defiant fear keeps green my whirling world.

Pow—Brave-O, my wise madmadam . . . Come, we'll lock away, and
mate again on Judgment Day.

*They Walk Out.*

Wom—Content—but I shall keep the key.

*She Locks Up.*

Pow—Content—I'll have the skeleton.

Wom—And I—a life.

# II. NORTH STAR WEST

*MARITIME FACES*

AS the waters grey, grace meets you
but only in gulls that hook on the wind
are shaken easily loose
curve to the curving wave

Not these the mark of Canada
nor yet the sentry beat of bergs
between each fortress fog your ship salutes
but here where heads of Hebridean mould
toss in crusted dories, hard fingers
sift dour living from the amber fins
that fleck these longdrowned Banks

Smell now the sweet landsmell, the spruce in the wind
but note, remember, how boxer waves
bully our shores, battling and billowing
into the stone's weakness, bellowing
down the deepening caverns
smashing the slate with unappeasable fists.

See these crouched hills at bay with Boreas
the old laconic resourceful hills
Something of this in the Maritime faces

THERE was the star of course
over the Gatineau hills
sudden and bright as a god
In the commotion, three Vice-Marshalls
roared to the air in pursuit
But it was only a *nova* in *Virgo*
betraying some cosmic tantrum
that ended a million years back
In a week the sky looked safe
and the astronomers' charts were mended


That shy chanting from clouds
heard by the Cardston cowpunchers
was found to be freakish "backlash"
from our shortwave station in Sackville


Jean-Baptiste le Sauvage
created some stir for a while
His followers opened their rooms to the roomless
and the Housing Commission was pleased
but when he mailed pamphlets to soldiers
—"Do violence to no one"—the usual line
the Wild Man from Rimouski
was jailed and forgotten
bearskin trousers and all
But then the Security Council
suddenly fell to agreeing
and the great glistening rockets were buried at sea
and the Rumour spread

And when with their wives and cameras
the Supreme Soviet and the U.S. Cabinet
went touring the world together
(icecream, folders, and great sheepish grins)
and none could be found to defame the Jews
and faces on streets began opening like flowers
we knew it was true

that somewhere again there had been a Birth
and Christmas . . . Christmas . . .
could be any day every day now and forever!

## PAGE OF GASPÉ

BETWEEN over-generous margins
between the unprinted river and the erased peaks
run the human typelines:
croplines freshening to the water
farms split to sentences by editor death
fattening subtitles of rockfence, rowan
and roads the covered bridges have clamped
like caught snakes

In this repetitive prose a sawmill
sets quote-marks after the stone windmill's period
and a Norman rubric
of rainbow skirts
flowers by a belltower grown from the woodcut village
But a later hand has added above the oxcart
two squat banks and an oblong factory

Daily now over the Gaspé landpage
grown-up children scribble
the smoke of transient trains
and the final shadows of jetplanes

## NORTH STAR WEST

*Montreal-Toronto*

IN a dazzle of lights and goodbyes
one by human one we mount our metal Ark
dryly escaping the flood of our days


But when doors clamp we are forty sly warriors
stowing briefcase ammunition for some Trojan target
merger-bombs for Bay Street, assault by speech in Winnipeg
(bright in the matched bags forward the Amazonian armour
awaiting some Vancouver beach-head)
Strapping ourselves to soft seats and softer magazines
we fix the individual light, the common thought


Snorts through four great nostrils Bellerophon's stallion
roars him seven thousand strong
trembles, moves like a cloud on the runway, wheels—
charges the night


Ah, we are speechless with life as it should be
our destinies fixed but our seats adjustable
airvents personal, discretion quite general
we lie like lambs in the lion of science
Time but a message now passed from our Pilot Gods
and tied to our button's touch
O Stewardess lively-loveliest
See her go gardening all up the aisle
blossoming every woolly head on a calyx of pillow
planting white bottles by the rockwalls of mothers
growing a border of trays and smiles
and yet herself is deftest flower of all

53

Loosed, lost from speed to undulating space
where the moon—below?—is boat longdrowned
and phosphorescent on the air's Atlantic ooze
and we some deepsea noser with a manta back
that cruises belly up toward a surge of clouds
Each wing's a twin of pilot sharks iridescent
each cowl runs photophores of hot and lambent blue
and ever like haloes the whirling antennae explore the night's abyss


". . . Over Brockville . . . Air speed 312 . . . Height 10,000 . . .
Temperature at ground, 80.   Outside, 6 below . . ."
The salesman with a face all yawn
hangs stockinged feet, limp flags of boredom, on the aisle
Free Life, free thought
and free electric shavers for the sanded jaw


Unseen the god-lips whisper through wires
their fingers play on a glittering loom of dials
weaving patterns of power and caution
Dreaming we sink to a galaxy, glide
are caught bat-footed in Toronto's hair

*Toronto-Winnipeg*

Like jungle-bright parrots migrating
the jangling colours and clouds of the dawn overtake us
snuffing the dew-bead lights of the farmhouse kitchens
filling the sky with the cry of the day
Poised and posed we lean to a reel of elms and barns
washed clean by height and light as models fixed for a Fair
orchards platonic, waterways swaying like tunes
and every town as charming as a child's new game

Lake now, sized to match its continent
and after Lake, lakes, lakes, like the plash of vanished saurians
that fought across an empire of green turf
fought and trampled till their slaty toemarks trod
the land to a thin net of bush flung on a world of water
Lakes and forever lakes, then—dim and miraculous as Martian lines—
the straight infinite prairie roads
and in one curving reach we clasp all Winnipeg

Ten cheeping crates of chicks, two nuns
the re-shod salesman and a hoard of mail
are sent about their earthly business

*Winnipeg-Edmonton*

O now we take a prairie in our glide
in the sky's wide room unroll a rug
of olive grain, of rivers worked in willowgreen,
of alkali-embroidered sloughs and flowered ponds
and the straight unending seams of road
With what airy eye we tighten the splayed village
absolve each whistle-stop of dust and heat
and trace clean sawdust rings around the lumbering suburb

Cloud-souls at first, moving reluctantly back
then a heaven of nothing sheets and shuts us to ourselves
Wingtips dissolve, propellers are thistledown
rain is a wind of water over the windows

The seated Fates in the ship's brain whisper each other
murmur a hundred leagues to the airport Olympus
Eyes read the pulse of a heart powered to a continent's leap
hands touch and tauten the nerve-ends of flight
A forty ton bubble we rise, rise,
break through clouds like rollers
burst to a sunlight five miles high

55

## North Star West

The professor overbids and goes down three
His mother orders buttered scones and tea

Cloudless again the plains lie like a slide in our microscope
amoebic with lakes, forests like fuzzed protozoan
A mile of contour-ploughing makes its thumbprint on the glass

Leaf-soft and slow we descend and descending stare
in the new Albertan landface that suntanned and open as ever
is pigtailed swarthy with oilsmoke and amber earringed with flame

Edmonton grows like a puzzled frown
Down, down, the eye-mote of our shadow widens to wingshape
like a butterfly rises to mate us

In the airport's queer solidity
men wear stetsons with stolidity
Honeymooners run for the plane
and the runway's caught in a ricey rain

*Edmonton-Vancouver*

Suddenly the coulees rush widening darkening to canyons
and we are a gull whirring alone
on a snowfrothed ocean of mountains
South to the humped breakers of Waterton our eyes
like planets roam, are held to the pronged wave of Assiniboine
pass to the tilted floes of Columbia's icefields
and beyond to Robson a foam on the northernmost swell
Yet always and swift as thinking we western
west over Kimberley's orestained trough
the caverned blues of the grizzled Kootenays, Windermere's jade
west and straight for a pearly wall like a homing angel
O but that Greenland of cloud buries the Rockies beneath us
and only the great berg of Baker turns afar in the sea-misted sun

56

Roaring and soft as a waterfall down from the timeless
we swoop to the Fraser, lassooing Vancouver's noon in the arc of our
    turn
We sink and are stayed
on the pitiless hardness of earth
Billboards and baggage checks master us
headlines open old wounds,
we bruise in a cabfull of cares to the city

Yet for a space we held in our morning's hand
the welling and wildness of Canada, the fling of a nation
We who have ridden the wings of our people's cunning
and lived in a star at peace among stars
return to our ferment of earth with a memory of sky

# THE MONARCH OF THE ID

*(With apologies to Gilbert but none to the Examiner
of Publications in the Customs Branch, Ottawa)*

## I

I am the scourge of scribbling crooks,
The Examiner of Books,
Whose might is right by the Customs Act.

*Chorus*

He bans every magazine of fiction or of fact,
Every drawing pornographic, every snap or pious tract,
All etchings, paintings, pamphlets, every artifact,
He bans every volume leather bound or paperbacked—
that fails to pass his quizz in Moral Tact!

## II

For all my salary is earned
Letting no page go unturned
To spot sedition, sex or treason.

*Chorus*

Whether masking as a classic or a book of rhyme or reason
Or a portrait of a lady who has not enough to please on,
He will stop them at the border and declare them out of season,
He will stamp them as fit only for Her Majesty's adhesion,
And obscene and full of blasphemy and treason!

## III

Anonymous in Ottawa
I preserve the Moral Law
And impound every drop of foreign sin.

*Chorus*

Neither Lawrence, Farrell, Faulkner, B. McFadden or their kin,
Neither Hanley, Patchen, Joyce, *Arabian Nights* or notes therein,
Neither Panter-Downes nor Radclyffe-Hall (although as yet *East Lynne*),
Neither Balzac, Edmund Wilson, Mailer, Maupassant or Glyn,
Henry Miller, Stopes or Trotsky, Margaret Sanger or Rubin,
May import or smuggle in their verbal gin!


IV

I am the Monarch of the Id,
The keeper of the Freudian Lid,
Though my praise no man or woman chants.

*Chorus*

Although all things immoral he can cipher at a glance
and singlehanded keeps us clothed in literary pants
There's none at home nor yet abroad who honours him with chants,
Except our Cabinet Ministers, their brothers in the Manse,
Their sisters and their cousins, whom they reckon up by dozens, and
    their aunts!

## RESTRICTED AREA

Stranger be warned, our land is queer
where Nature smiles the most, have fear
You may be just the one in thirty
with whom the whitest beach plays dirty
You may have just that gait in walking
which sets our tallest hostels rocking

A certain curvature of nose
may find a campus elm allergic
Some tint of skin or name or clothes
some breath or gesture thaumaturgic
can set the roofs of suburbs leaking
bands discording, golfers shrieking

Please understand it isnt mine
but Nature's whim to keep them lonely
All I can do is tack this sign
  FOR GENTILES ONLY

# BALLAD OF MR. CHUBB

O Mr. Chubb sells *Chubbsidized*
*Cars on Terms*
His RUMBLE IN   ROCKET OUT ! ! ! has quite outsized
nextdoor's neon *P e r m s*
not to speak
of the farmer's wooden WOᴙMS
beyond the town's fouled creek
        between two flowing hills in Minnesota


Across the sizzling highway O abandoned Mr. Chubb
likes to look
at each skirted golfing dub
who goes legging it over
S L I M ' S   H O O K
ᴀɴᴅ   S L I C E   C L I N I C
        beside a flaxblue lake in Minnesota


Mauve loudspeakers
over the PA
and MA
*C o m f o r t   S t a t i o n*   try to keep
Mr. Chubb O in whistle
with tunes expanding like thistle
from the goldgrey
jukebox of the *H O M E   S W E E T*
*H O M E B U R G E R   C A F E*
        by the blue flax-fields of Minnesota


But Mr. Chubb worries
of auto strikes as he hurries
with his cash and his daughter
past weedy

farms and cemeteries
to his lonely week-
end *" Bide-a-wee"*
       beside a sand-dune shore in Minnesota


And Mr. Chubb's cursed
with a fear and a fever
—O not that Lena wont live with him either—
but RUSSIA MAY DROP H-BOMB FIRST
before he's dug, dug, against the worst,
a leadlined shelter
       beneath his private hill in Minnesota


Yet all this hubbub
is wasted in Chubb.
With a hook and a slice
forbidden Slim
and flaxeyed Lena tonight
will strike to end all strikes
and dig him a worm-
lined home without terms
       under the waving nettles of Minnesota


Under the golfers' curves
O the jukebox stilled in his mind
Mr. Chubb will headlined
lie ASLEEP IN JESUS while
with her murderous lover
Mr. Chubb's perm-waved Lena
rockets far away and over
       the flaxen hills of Minnesota

## BUSHED

He invented a rainbow but lightning struck it
shattered it into the lake-lap of a mountain
so big his mind slowed when he looked at it

Yet he built a shack on the shore
learned to roast porcupine belly and
wore the quills on his hatband.

At first he was out with the dawn
whether it yellowed bright as wood-columbine
or was only a fuzzed moth in a flannel of storm
But he found the mountain was clearly alive
sent messages whizzing down every hot morning
boomed proclamations at noon and spread out
a white guard of goat
before falling asleep on its feet at sundown

When he tried his eyes on the lake, ospreys
would fall like valkyries
choosing the cut-throat
He took then to waiting
till the night smoke rose from the boil of the sunset

But the moon carved unknown totems
out of the lakeshore
owls in the beardusky woods derided him
moosehorned cedars circled his swamps and tossed
their antlers up to the stars
Then he knew though the mountain slept, the winds
were shaping its peak to an arrowhead
poised

But by now he could only
bar himself in and wait
for the great flint to come singing into his heart

## TAKKAKAW FALLS

Jupiter, Thor, how he thunders!
High in his own cloud somewhere
smashes
explodes on her upslant ledges
arcs out foaming
falls fighting—
o roaring cold down-geyser—
falls
falls gyring, flings
rain rainbows like peacock flights
vaulting the valley
His own gale rends him
heads off spray-comets
that hurl from her taut cliff
shreds even his cataract core
juggles it
struggles—holds?
falls
ho
like Woden
Zeus
down
terrible the bolt of him
(writhing past firs
foamdrowned to skeletons)
the hissing iced-nebulae whirl of him
crashes
batters unstayable
batters bullthroated
life-lunging
Tak-
ka-
kaw
batters the brown throbbing thighs of his mountain.

*Takkakaw Falls*

    Out of mist meekly the stream.
    Milk-young he mewls in naked-green moss
    bruise-purple boulders;
    slickens to slope, pours
    silt-turbulent through pine, races
    whole to the Yoho, coils
    with Columbia
    wanders the ocean tundra
    climbs by sunladders slowly to
    storm
    glacier
    down
    to the
    spawning
    thunder

## BIOGRAPHY

AT ten the years made tracks
plumped and sprung with pine-needles

Gaining height, overlooked
rock balanced on ridges
swords of snow in cliffside

Twenty, he lay by the lake
the bright unpredictable book
gracefully bound in green
and riffled its pages for rainbow

Life was a pup-tent, ptarmigan
chased along simmering slopes
bannocks and bacon
Only the night-mists died at dawn

By thirty, he trudged above timber
peered over ice at the peaks

As they swung slowly around him
the veins of bald glaciers blackened,
white pulses of waterfalls
beat in the bare rockflesh

Before him at forty
a nunatak stood like a sundial
swiftly marked time in the snow

Later a lancet of rime
hissed from the heave of the massif
a shrill wind shouldered him
and he turned

## Biography

But tried without might
had lost the lake or his nerve
forgot all the trail-forks
knew at the end only
the ice knuckling his eyes

## IMAGES IN PLACE OF LOGGING

WHERE quiet slid
through needled vaulting
iron brontosaurs
have crashed and bred
The steelshagged wolves
have barked and buried
green bones where deer
had arching fed

Now they tally the pacifist firs, the prodigal
oliveskinned planters put down
on the casualty lists of comptometers, scatter
resisters and make on the seared earth
the white child's crisscross of matchsticks
Later the freshets will sluice every fireweed wreath
from the tombs of the roots, till the spruce survivors
cut off, raise reddening hands to revolver sun

By the dying creek
a thoughtless poplar
flies autumn flags
for a cancelled fête
The old cold slugs
the covert glaciers
hunch and withdraw
to the bleak arête

O follow the silken hollow shapes
of the clouds that go gliding the empty
rooms of the sky, around and above
the browning pulp of the peeled world
and the men and the metalled ants that multiply on the **dead core**

## CLIMBERS

ABOVE the last squeak-squeal of wheels
stench of the highest backlot
lithe climbers escape leaping
through fir where chipmunks whirl
Twilight swirls at their backs
magenta hills dissolve
in faces, they curl in crypts
where stone has shelled
and doze while spires snuff out in a goldfluff cloud
At dawn along cherry cliffs they stalk
glimpse the peak in a muskmelon sky
and are beetles on bright glaciers
that wake chewing their cud of rock
over striped walls by beryl lakes
Climbers leave birdsong and follow
the spoor of goat over blocking ramparts
seeing afar the chalkstreaks of canyons
At noon below, stentorian icefalls unroll
and the climbers move under barred old snow
silently go beyond worn icefields
up the horny neck of desolation
till their hands bleed from the spines of the crest
and they lie at the end of thrust
weak in weak air and a daze of sight
on the pointless point of the peak
And this is the beginning of space
where there is nothing to say and
nothing to do and time only
for clambering back to the lean
pig of a streetcar squealing

## ST. VALENTINE IS PAST

(St. Valentine is past; begin these wood-birds but to couple now?"
—*Midsummer Night's Dream.*)

WHEN Theseus wheels his high deaf back
  hallooing toward the boar
they turn like teal to summer sea
  beat wordless to their shore

She walks then like a waterfall
  like all a water failing
and she is subtle as her spray
  below the sunlight paling

While he is rooted rock she strikes
  to foam a loud cascade
that drowns the jeering gullish wings
  far crashings in the glade

No more while lizard minutes sleep
  around a cactus land
they'll blow their longings out like spores
  that never grass the sand

No longer Time's a cloud of cliffs
  unechoed by her Nile
he'll hide no more from suns that may
  elsewhere break out her smile

Daylong they watch their sky forget
  each old crow's winging shadow
'O we will build a dam of love
  and dapple all the meadow'

And yet and yet a failing rod
   strikes only dust from rock
while all the tune and time they breathe
   is never kept in talk


Now water sky and rock are gone
   the huddled woodbirds back
and hot upon the throbbing boar
   comes Theseus with his pack